Pak

in Indonesia

Text and photographs by Alain Chenevière

Translated by Lisa Davidson

Lerner Publications Company
Minneapolis

All words that appear in **bold** are explained in a glossary on page 58.

© Hachette Livre 1994. Originally produced as *Pak: L'enfant cocher* in 1994 by Hachette Livre, Paris, France. Text and photographs by Alain Chenevière.

Library of Congress Cataloging-in-Publications Data

Chenevière, Alain.
    [Pak, L'enfant cocher. English]
    Pak in Indonesia / by Alain Chenevière : translated by Lisa Davidson.
        p. cm. — (My future)
    Includes index.
    Summary: Describes the work of a young Indonesian bull driver who trains and races his animals and portrays the culture, geography, and economy if his country.
    ISBN 0–8225–2826–6 (lib. bdg.)
    1. Indonesia—Social life and customs—Juvenile literature. 2. Bull racing—Indonesia—Juvenile literature. 3. Children—Indonesia—Juvenile literature. [1. Indonesia. 2. Bull racing.] I. Davidson, Lisa. II. Title. III. Series.
DS625.C47713 1996
959.803—dc20
                                     95–31072
                                         CIP
                                         AC

Printed in France by I.M.E.
Bound in the United States of America
1 2 3 4 5 6 — 01 00 99 98 97 96

Contents

"Take a good look! His name is Aruan. I've never seen such a handsome animal," said the breeder. "But watch out, he's mean. Sometimes he pulls to the left without warning."

For the first time in his life, Pak found himself face to face with a Tanah Merah (Red Earth), one of the legendary Indonesian bulls he had dreamed about since he was a small child.

The brown animal snorted furiously and threw himself with all his force against the gate of the wooden fence. Pak jumped backwards. The bull stared at him with his small black eyes. His tail whipped back and forth wildly. He held his head high and his nostrils quivered in the bright light.

"What an incredible animal!" thought Pak.

He was impressed. He had just met the second animal of his team, the bull that would run alongside his Bondowoso (white bull) called Karang.

Pak, which means "little father," was a nickname. His real name was Hassan Moktar Lubis, and he lived in the small village of Kedunsung on the island of Madura. Pak was 13 years old, but the wrinkle on his forehead, his knitted brows, and his dark eyes made him seem more serious than other boys his age. He rarely smiled. It bored him to play with the other children.

Pak had earned his nickname because of his small size and because he walked slightly bent over. But under his timid appearance, the "little father" had a will of iron and a single passion—to race bulls.

Pak learned this love of racing from Amin, his older brother. When Pak was six years old, Amin took him to his first **kerapan sapi** (race with bulls harnessed to a shaft). The race amazed the boy. "One day," he thought, "I will ride these fabulous animals!"

Since that day, Pak had never left the world of the bulls. He started by cleaning stables. Then he was allowed to take care of the bulls. He learned to talk to them, care for them, and earn their respect. He was no longer afraid of the animals, who weighed more than 800 pounds.

With experience Pak became a racing specialist. He had already driven teams during the kerapan desa (small village races). And bulls were part of his family tradition. How many times had he heard the story of his great-grandfather Sayuddin, who lived to be 100 years old and devoted his entire life to breeding bulls? And because he was from Bondowoso, what other profession could he have chosen?

For anyone who loves bulls and water buffalo, Bondowoso is a mythical place.

This small village in eastern Java breeds the best bulls in the entire region. The animals are carefully selected and skillfully crossbred. Pak had made many trips to Bondowoso with his father and his uncles. He remembered every moment of these trips. He returned from these trips knowing that the Bondowoso were truly exceptional animals.

As Pak stood in front of the enormous black-eyed Tanah Merah, he told himself that only this animal could equal the Bondowoso. "A Tanah Merah is more powerful, but harder to train." Pak guessed that their reputation was well deserved.

The previous year, Pak's father, Tibor, had suggested teaming a Bondowoso with a Tanah Merah. No one took him seriously at first. But Tibor was a stubborn man. Pak could still hear him talking with his uncles, Umar and Ailsa. The boy was in bed in the next room and couldn't fall asleep.

"We will mix the fire of the 'red' with the wisdom of the 'white'. No one will be able to go faster!" his father had said.

But Uncle Ailsa objected immediately. "Nobody has ever been able to harness a Tanah Merah and a Bondowoso together."

"That's because they always let the Bondowoso lead the team, thinking he is more intelligent. That's not the right way. You have to trust the Tanah Merah and match his aggressiveness with the power of the other animal," replied Pak's father.

Then Uncle Umar raised an important question.

"Who will be able to control such a team and make it run in a straight line during the race? We need a driver who is strong enough to control the 'red,' flexible enough for the 'white,' yet light enough so the wagon won't be too heavy."

"But we have him!" Pak's father cried.

Pak gave a start as he heard his father say his name.

"Hassan, of course! He has been taking care of our bulls since he was eight years old. Did you see him at the races at Sampang? Three victories out of four races. He is light and strong. He knows these animals better than anyone. He talks to them, he understands them. With Pak and the team I'm suggesting, we can win the kerapan besar (championship race) in Pamekasan this fall. But we have to start training Hassan immediately to get him fit enough."

So the following day, Pak found himself facing the destiny that he had always dreamed of, and his life changed radically. From that day forward, he live in a world of men—eating, sleeping, drinking, and talking only to men. "Women and bulls don't mix!" his Uncle Umar often repeated. Pak's own mother avoided interfering in his life, afraid that she might disrupt his preparations.

The other major change was that Pak often missed school. But what child would complain about that? Pak knew what he would do if given the choice between stuffy classrooms and the freedom of the outdoors. And since his father's wishes matched his own secret desires, what a pleasure it was to obey him!

As Pak and his father looked at the Tanah Merah, the breeder slapped Pak on the back and said, "This is the boy who will lead you to victory, this one and none other!" Pak knew that the man spoke the truth.

They returned home. The Tanah Merah and the Bondowoso were placed together. Pak lived with them during training. He ate little and slept as few hours as possible. With Karang, everything went well. But Aruan didn't like the yoke. At first, when Pak finally managed to harness him, he galloped 100 yards at the same speed as Karang, then turned sharply to the left. It was a catastrophe every time—the cart somersaulted, and Pak flew head over heels. The huge bruises all over his body reflected the force of his falls.

Yet the boy had the courage of a great driver. Patiently, he wiped off his bumps and bruises and bandaged his wounds. Then he talked to his animals, calming them down. And he started over and over again. Little by little, his efforts were rewarded. The animals learned how to pull together, and the team grew to be very powerful.

"Will you make me win?" Pak wondered every night, as he watched his bulls.

But he didn't have time to doubt. Pak could only think about tomorrow. Tomorrow the qualification races began at Sumenep, in eastern Madura.

Pak won the race in Sumenep, and the twangy loudspeaker in the stadium blared, "Hassan Lubis of Kedunsung. Qualified!" Standing straight on the shaft between his bulls, Pak raised a fist to the sky. His first real victory!

The following week, Pak won at Konang, and the week after, at Semulu. Two weeks later, he finished second in the large stadium at Sampang.

People who followed the races began to talk about Hassan of Kedunsung, but Pak paid little attention. The only thing that mattered to him was his victory in the last two races, which meant he could participate in the kerapan kapubaten (a series of elimination races). Pak would need the time before the races to prepare, because the cooperation between Aruan and Karang was far from perfect.

The first round of the elimination races took place in Karangpinang. Although Aruan swerved during the race, frightening Pak, the team ran well.

"Hassan Lubis of Kedunsung wins!" screamed the speaker.

Amin and Tibor hurried over to congratulate Pak. Just as he was getting off his cart, happy and proud, he noticed a man watching him. The man was wearing a distinctive red and gold headband around his forehead. "A man from the island of Bali," thought Pak. "What's he doing here?" But just then, the stranger disappeared into the crowd, and Pak forgot about him.

Nine days later, at Tambelangar, Pak won the second round of the elimination races. His brother grabbed him from the cart and hoisted him onto his shoulders. With his arms raised in triumph, Pak looked at the winner's trophy his father was proudly holding up. Suddenly Pak noticed a familiar shape moving through the crowd that had gathered around him. It was the red headband—the Balinese, the man he had seen in Karangpinang. "There's that man again!" said the boy, surprised. But a second later, the Balinese disappeared.

A week and a half later, at Baliga, Aruan was up to his old tricks. Twenty yards from the finish line, he suddenly pulled with all his force to the left, toward the crowd. The impact was incredible. Pak found himself on the ground in the middle of a cloud of dust, spectators screaming on all sides. Two of them were hurt, and Pak suffered scratches and a deep cut in his shoulder. He was almost eliminated from the competition.

The worst thing was that the Bondowoso had injured his left knee and was limping badly. While the boy examined the animal, he felt someone watching him from behind. He turned around quickly. The Balinese was there, watching. Pak shrugged his shoulders. The man backed away.

In a month's time, Karang was in better shape and ran like before. The atmosphere in the stadium of Pakong that day was tense. Out of four races, only the two overall leaders would qualify for the next set of races.

Pak won the first two races easily. But he finished fifth in the third race because Aruan once again veered off. Fortunately,

Pak qualified in the last race by finishing second.

His father and his two uncles came to congratulate him.

"You just barely made it," said Tibor.

Pak didn't answer. He had been afraid that his Tanah Merah would ruin everything. He was angry at the bull, who had betrayed him for no reason. Alone with his animals, Pak saved his praise for the loyal Karang. A man came up to him. It was the Balinese, the man with the red headband. This time, Pak decided to find out what he really wanted. "Are you from Bali?"

"Yes . . . from Negara," answered the man.

Pak couldn't hide his surprise. Negara was a large town in western Bali, famous for the **mekepung** (races with buffalo harnessed to wagons).

"You're interested in karapan sapi?" asked Pak.

"Not just that," replied the Balinese with a smile.

"I've seen you several times," said Pak. "Did you come to see me or is it just a coincidence?"

"No. I came because of you."

"And why me? There are other drivers in Madura."

"There are others, yes, but you are the best. And I wanted to know more about the driver we're going to beat in Pamekasan."

"Who is 'we'?"

"You'll see soon enough," said the man shortly. "Let's just say that I know the person who will beat you."

Pak couldn't believe his ears.

"Is that right!" he exclaimed, his throat dry with anger. "You dare say that to a Maduran?"

But the man didn't press his point.

"See you soon!" he promised, with a sly smile on his face. And he left as quickly as he had appeared.

That evening an important meeting was held in Tibor's house. Pak and his father were seated in the middle of the room. Thirty men sat around them, including Pak's brother and his two uncles. Pak was worried and didn't let go of Amin's hand. Pak felt better knowing his brother was next to him. Amin spoke first.

"Who is this man?"

No one answered. A few men shrugged in response.

"What is he looking for?" continued Amin. "Why is he bothering Pak all the time?"

"Wait a minute," interrupted Uncle Ailsa. "This Balinese never really bothered Pak. He just let him know that Pak was going to face a champion!"

"And where does he plan to find this champion?" bellowed one of the men.

"We know all the best drivers!" added another. "They live here, on Madura!"

Everyone looked at Uncle Umar.

"Wrong!" he said. "There are excellent drivers elsewhere. Remember the Javanese who finished second in the kerapan besar in Pamekasan two years ago? There are champions on Bali as well, and their mekepung are not just pleasure rides!"

"But it's not the same thing!" roared Pak's father. "They have buffalo and wagons with wheels, and they race in a line, one behind the other. Here, the drivers have to balance on a single shaft pulled by crazed, angry bulls!"

But Umar was sure of himself. Very quietly, he said, "Their buffalo are as powerful as our bulls, and their races are extremely dangerous."

Pak knew that his father was worried. A heavy silence followed. Finally, Tibor made a decision.

"There's no use talking. We have to act. You, Ailsa, go find out about this man. Every time he comes to Madura, he stays at the Grand Hotel. I want to know who he is, where he comes from, and what he wants. You, Umar, go to Bali and try to find out about the best mekepung drivers. Their names, their ages, everything!"

Ten days later, everyone met again in Tibor's house. They had all the information

Tibor wanted. Ailsa revealed that the mysterious Balinese was named Njoman Ketut. He was a rich landowner from a small town near Negara. He owned one of the best breeding farms of racing buffalo in all of Bali. But Ailsa saved the most important news for last. At great expense, the Balinese was training a man named Baduwesa.

"Baduwesa!" cried Uncle Umar.

"Do you know him?" asked Tibor.

"Do I know him? He's all they talk about in Negara. He's an incredible driver!"

Uncle Umar described his two visits to Bali in detail. He had watched four mekepung and was extremely impressed by the ferociousness of these races. He had only seen the famous Baduwesa once but knew right away that he was a serious competitor. He was unmatched as a driver, possessing all the pride and confidence that make a real champion. Only 19 years old, Baduwesa had already won three championships in four years. This year, he had decided to compete against Indonesia's best—the Maduran. And he was going to do it on their own island, where they had never been beaten before! He had so much self-confidence that he swore to everyone he would bring the trophy back to Bali.

The group was silent. Many people lowered their heads. Pak didn't dare say anything. He wanted to tell them that he wasn't afraid—that he, too, was confident of his talent. All the drivers he'd competed against had been excellent drivers. Was Baduwesa any different?

One hot summer Friday, while Pak was rubbing down his animals, Tibor arrived. His father looked worried. "Pak," he said, "I have to talk to you. Do you remember Njoman from Bali and Baduwesa?"

Of course Pak remembered.

"I found out that they are going to participate in the mekepung semifinals in western Bali next Sunday," continued Tibor. "I thought it would be a good idea if we all went to see him."

"Why is that?" asked Pak.

"Well, your uncles and I think it would be good for you to see how he drives, know how he works. To see what he's like."

"I'll do whatever you want," said Pak.

He felt a slight twinge. Why did his family doubt him? Why did they fear Baduwesa so much?

Pak discovered the answers to his questions the following Sunday. He had just watched a series of violent mekepung, which pitted powerful teams against one another in the midst of rice paddies. Shimmering banners blazed and buffalo hooves thundered over the ground. Pak saw the enormous gray and pink buffalo finish the races completely exhausted, their sides and nostrils bloodied. He saw the drivers collapse as they crossed the finish line. And he saw Baduwesa.

Baduwesa dominated every event with his strong will to triumph. He won everything and roared with every victory. Baduwesa knew he was the best. He wanted everyone else to know it, too!

A big crowd surrounded the hero of the day as the trophies were distributed. Pak moved closer to Baduwesa, who was stroking his trophy. The young man was tall and well proportioned. His long curly hair had slipped out of the purple headband that circled his bulging forehead. His small eyes didn't seem to have any whites in them at all. They moved constantly, as if he were watching his prey. Thin lips and a square jaw completed the picture of this champion. His entire face breathed energy and the will to win. Two hands suddenly lifted the trophy from Baduwesa to show it to the crowd of supporters. It was Njoman, with his red headband. He suddenly turned to look at Pak. Instinctively, the boy hid behind one of the spectators.

"Did he see me?" he wondered, feeling ashamed like a small child caught spying. Embarrassed, Pak backed away and joined his father and uncles, who were waiting for him.

"So, did you see him?" questioned his father.

"See who?"

"You know very well who I'm talking about!"

"Yes, I saw him," admitted Pak.

"And?"

"And? He's a great champion."

"That's all?" insisted Tibor.

"Yes, that's all."

Pak's tone of voice surprised his father. The two uncles didn't say a word. It was time to leave to go back home to Madura.

Pak easily won the elimination races held in June and July in his district. Now it was time for the kapubaten (regional races). The winners went from there to the kerapan besar held in Pamekasan, Madura's capital, in the fall.

Pak won everything, even though Aruan once again veered off and almost hit the crowd. After the race, Pak remained for a long time with his bull. He spoke to him about loyalty, honor, and friendship, while stroking his neck. The animal listened without moving. Did he understand the words of his young master?

Time passed quickly. Finally, the day of the long-awaited races arrived. At ten o'clock, the teams would start racing in groups of seven or eight. The winner of each race would go on to the finals. By five o'clock, the event would be over, and the winner of the kerapan besar would be the hero of the day.

For more than a week, an atmosphere of crazy excitement reigned over Pamekasan. The population had increased tenfold, and people were sleeping in tents and on the streets. Police and soldiers were everywhere. Shops stayed open all night long, and people were singing and dancing in the streets. **Gamelans** (traditional Indonesian orchestras) played on every corner. Parades passed by, and the voices of people betting on the races mixed with the laughter of children.

Like the other drivers, Pak was kept carefully away from the festive town. His family took care to protect him so that nothing would upset him before the race.

On the morning of the race, Pak got out of bed. He had spent the night tossing and turning and had not slept a wink. All he could think about was the race with Baduwesa. He decided to go see his bulls.

19

Nothing was moving as he crossed the courtyard. He pushed open the door of the stables. Multicolored garlands and wreaths decorated every inch of the stables from floor to ceiling. Red and green flags hung on the wall, and bouquets of flowers overflowed near the feeding trough. Eggs, honey, medicinal plants, and other special offerings were placed on the floor in front of the bulls.

Karang was lying on his side and turned his head when Pak appeared. Aruan was standing up. Pak walked over to see him first. He placed his hand on the animal's forehead. He looked deeply into Aruan's eyes and spoke to him.

"Today, Red, I need you. I haven't been able to get to really know you. You are stronger than any other animal, but you are also the most unpredictable. Maybe I have hurt you without knowing it, and you want to make me pay by not always obeying me. But today, you can't let us down, Karang and me. Please, lead us to victory today. No matter if we win or we lose, we do it together as a team."

Aruan did not move, but Karang stood up. Pak put his arm around the neck of each of his animals and said again, "Whatever happens, I did my best." And he planted a kiss on the forehead of each bull.

The final was about to start. Hassan Moktar Lubis, son of Tibor Lubis, great-grandson of Sayuddin Lubis, was standing on the shaft of his red and green wagon. His bare feet clenched the rough wood. He wore a colorful red and green T-shirt over a pair of black shorts. Nervous, he shivered despite the sweltering heat.

Massages by his mother had not managed to relax Pak. After rubbing perfumed oil on her son, she carefully wrapped his ankles with bands. Then she held him tightly in her arms. When he pulled away, Pak noticed that her eyes were wet.

At the racetrack, his father tied a yellow headband for good luck around Pak's forehead, then hoisted him up to the wagon. He didn't say a word. Nor did Amin and the two uncles, who remained in the background, watching Pak encouragingly. They were all anxious.

Pak surveyed the racetrack in front of him. The grass was burned dry by the hot summer sun. About 150 yards ahead, he could just make out the simple chalk finish line. The judges' stand and timers stood to the right of the finish line.

A cloud of dust floated above the track. The seven qualifying teams of bulls had just paraded triumphantly before the crowd of enthusiastic spectators. The painted horns of the enormous beasts were hung with bells. The animals were draped with cloth bearing the colors of their owners, who were each walking proudly beside their beasts.

In minutes the bulls were harnessed to their shafts. The track was cleared, and the drivers arrived. Each driver was cheered as the possible hero of the day. In two minutes, the race would start.

All the bulls were stamping their feet, at the peak of excitement. Pak was having difficulty balancing on the shaft, which his crazed bulls were knocking about wildly. The men clustered around the teams were barely able to keep the bulls at the starting line.

The judges raised their red flags. Pak turned to the right to look at Baduwesa, who was three teams away. He seemed calm. He was looking straight ahead and hardly noticed the jostling of his team. Suddenly, silence fell over the crowded stadium. Everyone in the crowd held his breath.

"Five! Four! Three! Two! One! Oooooohhh!" screamed the loudspeaker.

Pak saw the red flags drop just as the trainers' whips smacked the bulls' hindquarters.

Braced on the shaft, Pak pulled the tails of his animals downward to spur them onward, just as he had been taught to do. A nearby team fell and one of the bulls rolled in the dust. The team's wagon flew into the air, then bounced on the ground.

The mad race continued. Pak could no longer control the movement of the shaft. He held onto the reins and clenched his teeth. The scenery and the spectators seemed to rush past him. He thought he was in the lead, but he wasn't sure. Too fast! Too much dust! The rows of spectators ahead began to make way for the teams. "The finish line!" thought Pak.

At that moment, Pak felt the presence of Baduwesa, whose team was even with his. A scream of rage burst from Pak's lungs. He would never let himself be beaten by a Balinese! "Aruan! Aruan!" he yelled. The enormous animal lengthened his stride, pulling Karang along. But Baduwesa's bulls were also in a fury to win. Side by side, neither of the teams backed down. Pak and Baduwesa were focused on the finish line, which was getting closer rapidly. Neither one slowed down. Each of them knew how dangerous it would be to bring their team to a stop at such fast speeds. Many careless drivers had lost their lives this way.

The two teams crossed the finish line together. "Now!" cried Pak. He leaped over the yoke to stop his bulls. At that same moment, beside himself with exhaustion, Karang suddenly veered to the right. Pak fell over the yoke, which shot him into the air like a puppet. He yelled, "Not you Karang! No, not you!" then crashed to the ground as the crowd screamed and yelled. And then, nothing but blackness.

Carried by his father, Pak didn't know yet that he had won the final race at Pamekasan. He had won by just a nose—that of Aruan, "the red!"

Pictures

In Indonesia, fields are gradually replacing tropical forests, which once covered all the islands. Volcanoes erupt from time to time, enriching the soil with their ash.

Rice paddies climb up the sides of mountains, which have been terraced over the centuries. Women are often responsible for planting the rice seedlings.

Agriculture employs about 60 percent of the population in Indonesia, where farming is practiced with traditional techniques and tools. Indonesian farmers rely on humidity and the exceptional fertility of the soil for their crops.

Balancing on a single shaft, a driver leads two bulls to victory at a kerapan sapi in Madura. The animals run at speeds of more than 40 miles per hour.

The mekepung *(top left)* and the kerapan sapi *(bottom left)* attract huge crowds.

About 198 million people live in Indonesia,

including more than 350 ethnic groups

scattered throughout the archipelago (group of islands).

Notebook

Geography

1

A World Apart

Indonesia is a Southeast Asian country located between the Indian Ocean and the South China Sea. The country is made up of more than 13,000 islands, including Java, Sumatra, Kalimantan, and Sulawesi *(map 1)*.

The vast region that encompasses the island of Madura, the eastern part of Java, and the western part of Bali *(map 2)* is known as the "region of the bulls." The region, which covers a surface area of about 17,760 square miles, is divided lengthwise by the Barisan Mountains. A continuation of the central mountain chain on the island of Sumatra, the Barisan Mountains cross Java and extend to islands farther east. On either side of the mountains, high plateaus give way to coastal plains.

Republic of Indonesia
Capital: Jakarta
Surface area: 741,098 square miles
Currency: rupiah
Languages: Bahasa Indonesia (official) plus 200 regional languages and dialects.

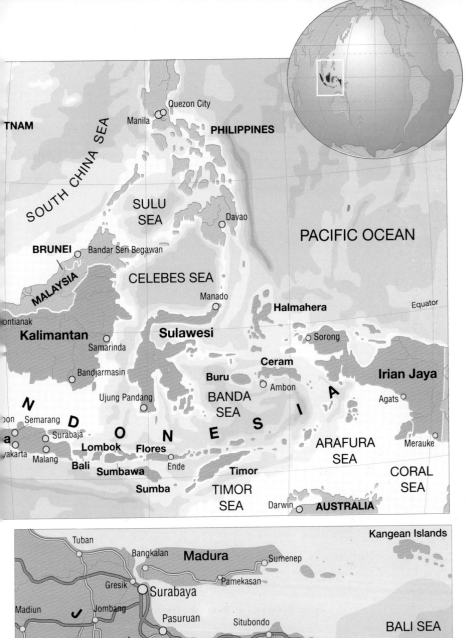

TNAM

SOUTH CHINA SEA

Manila ○
Quezon City ○

PHILIPPINES

SULU SEA

Davao ○

PACIFIC OCEAN

BRUNEI ○ Bandar Seri Begawan

MALAYSIA

CELEBES SEA

Manado ○

Halmahera

Equator

ontianak ○

Kalimantan

Samarinda ○

Sulawesi

○ Sorong

Irian Jaya

Bandjarmasin ○

Ceram

○ Ambon

Agats ○

Ujung Pandang ○

Buru

BANDA SEA

N

D

O

N

E

S

I

A

ARAFURA SEA

Merauke ○

oon ○

Semarang ○

Surabaja ○

Lombok

Flores

Ende ○

Timor

CORAL SEA

yakarta ○

Malang ○

Bali

Sumbawa

Sumba

TIMOR SEA

Darwin ○ **AUSTRALIA**

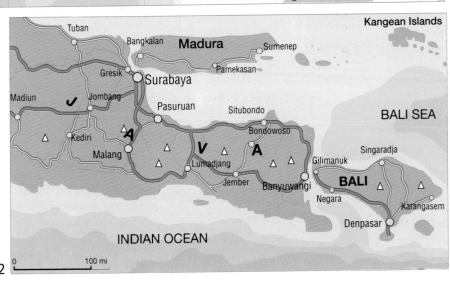

Tuban ○

Bangkalan ○

Madura

Sumenep ○

Kangean Islands

Gresik ○

Pamekasan ○

Surabaya

Madiun ○

Jombang ○

Pasuruan

Situbondo

BALI SEA

Kediri ○

Bondowoso

Malang ○

Lumadjang ○

Singaradja ○

Jember ○

Banyuwangi

Gilimanuk

BALI

Negara

Karangasem

Denpasar ○

INDIAN OCEAN

0   100 mi

2

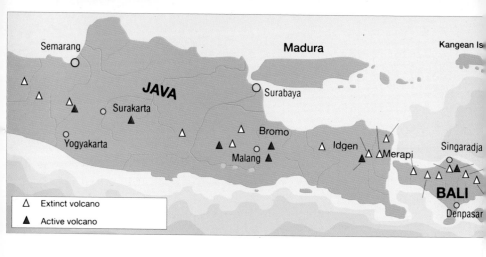

Map labels:
Semarang, Madura, Kangean Is, JAVA, Surabaya, Surakarta, Yogyakarta, Bromo, Idgen, Merapi, Singaradja, Malang, BALI, Denpasar

△ Extinct volcano
▲ Active volcano

A Volcanic Region

Indonesia's major features are its rugged landscape and its intense volcanic activity, particularly on Java and Bali. Of more than 400 volcanoes in Indonesia, 112 are on Java, including 35 that are still active. Located in eastern Java, Merapi, for example, erupts approximately every five years. The ash ejected by the volcanoes create extremely fertile soil. Bali has four volcanoes.

Located in eastern Java, Bromo Volcano, which rises 7,546 feet, may erupt at any moment.

Indonesian Plants and Animals

Left to right: buffalo, crocodile, and the endangered Asian tiger.

40

Key Facts

- Indonesia has more than 13,000 islands.
- Some of the country's many volcanoes are still active.
- The "region of the bulls" covers about 17,760 square miles.
- Most of the islands are covered with tropical rain forests.

Constant Humidity

The islands of Indonesia sit near the equator and receive constant rains, as well as northern **monsoons** from December until March. In fact, Indonesia has only two seasons—wet and wetter. The average temperature is around 79° F.

The islands' abundant rainfall created thick forests. But on Java, on Madura, and particularly on Bali, intensive farming has destroyed almost all tree cover. As a result, the soil has become much less fertile. Some farming experts even predict that the "region of the bulls" will become a vast desert by the year 2020.

Fewer Forests

The "region of the bulls" has lost almost all of its original forests. But dense tropical rain forests still cover many Indonesian islands, particularly Kalimantan.

Dense tropical forest still carpets many Indonesian islands.

Coconut palm   Bamboo   Oil palm   Hevea

41

People and Their Work

Indonesia's Population

About 198 million people live in Indonesia. Although the birthrate has fallen, the population continues to grow at a rate of almost 2 percent each year. This is partly due to a longer life expectancy, which is 63 years, and by a steep drop in infant mortality.

Most Indonesians are **Malays.** Other groups include the Papuan, who live on Irian Jaya (the western part of the island

of New Guinea), and the descendants of **Negritos**—an Asian people who came to the Indonesian archipelago thousands of years ago.

These different peoples arrived over time from central China and established settlements in the archipelago between 4,500 and 2,000 years ago. A distinction is sometimes made between the Proto-Malays (the first Malays) and the Deutero-Malays (the second Malays). The first group preserved its ancestral social and religious systems, remaining somewhat removed from the

modern world. The second group converted to major world religions, especially Islam.

Modern Indonesia has numerous ethnic groupings. Besides the Javanese, who make up more than 80 percent of the total population, 350 additional ethnic groups live on the islands of the archipelago.

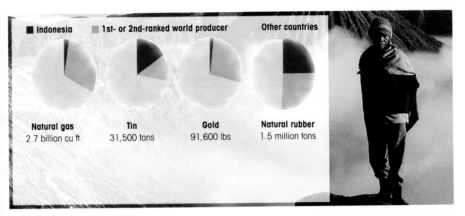

Natural gas	Tin	Gold	Natural rubber
2.7 billion cu ft	31,500 tons	91,600 lbs	1.5 million tons

■ Indonesia   ■ 1st- or 2nd-ranked world producer   □ Other countries

Natural Wealth

Indonesia has a wealth of natural resources, but paying off a large national debt takes up a significant part of the country's income. Nevertheless, Indonesia is slowly developing its resources. Energy production alone produces approximately $13 billion a year. Indonesia also has abundant supplies of oil, natural gas, coal, tin, nickel, copper, bauxite, manganese, gold, and silver.

In addition, agriculture accounts for 25 percent of Indonesia's income. Indonesian farm products include rice, tea, coffee, soybeans, and rubber. And if the country continues to increase its export of raw materials, particularly oil and gas, Indonesia may have a balanced economy in the near future.

Idjen, a volcanic mountain on eastern Java, produces huge amounts of sulfur. Workers labor in the sulfur mines for very low wages.

What Lies Ahead?

Indonesia earns a lot of money from the sale of oil. As the nation continues to develop its resources, it may become one of the most important economies of Asia in the 21st century. With a

low standard of living, however, most Indonesians will probably not become wealthy.

43

In Indonesia, men till the fields, and women harvest crops.

An Agricultural Society

Farming in Indonesia employs close to 60 percent of the population. The economy is based on agriculture because of the fertility of the soil, the excellent climatic conditions, and the increasing needs of a growing population. Almost all the land on Java, Madura, and Bali is now farmed.

Major crops are rice, corn, sweet potatoes, soybeans, cassavas, peanuts, sugarcane, copra, tea, and coffee. Indonesia is among the top world producers of latex, a natural fluid from which rubber is made.

Ranchers raise large herds of cattle and sheep. Some of the breeds are highly prized for racing and fighting. The "region of the bulls" is home to about two-thirds of these ranches.

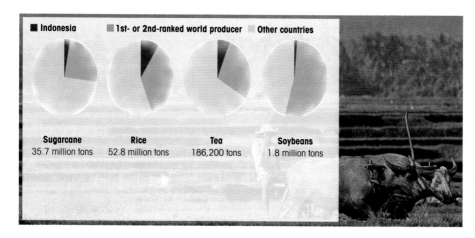

■ Indonesia   ▨ 1st- or 2nd-ranked world producer   ▨ Other countries

Sugarcane	Rice	Tea	Soybeans
35.7 million tons	52.8 million tons	186,200 tons	1.8 million tons

Rice

Mountainside rice paddies dominate Indonesia's landscape. As in other Asian countries, rice is the staple food in Indonesia, which is one of the world's biggest rice-producing countries. Rice makes up about one-fourth of the country's grain production. Small altars dedicated to the spirits of the land are placed almost everywhere throughout the countryside to protect the precious crops.

Indonesians can harvest two or even three rice crops each year because of the country's climate and fertile soil.

Hevea

The hevea tree whose milky latex is used for making rubber, was introduced in Indonesia in the 1800s. The slender trunk of the hevea tree is topped by a bushy clump of leaves. The tree requires fertile soil and constant humid heat of around 77° F, producing latex only after six years of growth. During the dry season, workers cut into the trunk so the latex will drip into a bucket attached to the tree. The liquid is then blackened with smoke to stick together, creating blocks of rubber that are sent to industrial treatment plants. Between 660 and 880 pounds of natural rubber can be produced on 2.5 acres of hevea trees.

History

Ancient Past

Some scientists believe that the "region of the bulls" was one of the first inhabited areas of Indonesia. Approximately 40,000 years ago, nomadic peoples hunted and gathered their food in the thick forests that once covered the land. By the 1400s B.C., descendants of the hunter-gatherers began to raise buffalo and to grow rice in permanent villages.

Epic stories from India that date to the sixth century B.C. mention the existence of an important cultural region, with Java as its center. In the A.D. 400s, the Chinese Buddhist monk Fa-hsien was shipwrecked on Java and later wrote about the civilization he saw there. During the second century A.D., trade links had been established between Indonesia and India. For more than 1,000 years, India had strong economic, political, and religious influence over the western half of the archipelago. Merchants brought goods from India. The Hindu faith, practiced in India, also made its way to the islands.

Indian Influences

Indian-influenced kingdoms, governed by rulers who had converted to the Hindu religion, had developed in Sumatra and in central Java by the seventh century A.D. A power struggle quickly sprang up between the Sumatrans and the Javanese for control of the Indonesian islands.

A gamelan, or Indonesian orchestra.

Dugout canoes on Fondono Lake.

Emergence of Eastern Java

The Sumatrans triumphed over the Javanese, especially under the reign of the great Indo-Buddhist empire of Srivijaya (600s–1200s A.D.). When western Java fell under its control, the Javanese leaders fled to the eastern side of the island and began a long war to reconquer the island. In 1222 one of the exiled Javanese kings, Ken Angrok, extended his authority throughout all of eastern Java. His successors took over Madura and Bali.

Fightings the Mongols

After the collapse of the Srivijaya Empire in the 1200s, Javanese kings faced internal conflict. At the same time, Mongol groups from the Yuan dynasty (family of rulers) in China invaded the archipelago. After a long war, Javanese troops defeated the Mongols. The victorious king, Raden Widjaya, then founded the kingdom of Madjapahit in 1294.

The Madjapahit Kingdom

Within a few years, the Madjapahit kingdom had become the region's greatest military, commercial, and cultural power. The Madjapahit court attracted artists and scholars from all over Asia. By the mid-1300s, the Madjapahit kingdom dominated all of Indonesia and parts of the neighboring Malay Peninsula.

The Madjapahit kingdom traded with China, Taiwan, and all the islands in the region. Madjapahit was eventually conquered by Muslims, who practiced the religion of Islam.

47

(Left) *The sultan of Yogyakarta, Java.* (Facing page top) *The governor of the Moluccas (islands in eastern Indonesia) offered wild hogs to the French explorer Jules Dumont d'Urville during his visit in the early 1800s.*

The Arrival of Europeans

A new chapter in Indonesian history opened with the arrival of Europeans in the early 1500s. The first to reach the islands were the Portuguese, followed shortly after by the Spanish. The Dutch arrived from the Netherlands in the 1600s, taking control of almost all the Indonesian islands. In 1602 the Dutch East India Company was formed, and it held a monopoly in the Indonesian spice trade until the late 1600s. A long, bloody struggle took place between the Dutch and the sultans during

Era of the Sultans

The religion of Islam, which had been present in the Indonesian archipelago since the 700s, gradually gained in influence throughout the islands. Sultans (Islamic leaders) overturned the Hindu kings one after another, conquering the Madjapahit kingdom by the early 1500s. Since then Islam has been the major religion throughout all of Indonesia.

Modern Times

the 1700s. The increasing influence of the British in Asia contributed to the collapse of the Dutch East India Company. In 1814 and again in 1824, Britain and the Netherlands signed trading and military agreements, dividing the country between them.

Dutch ships

In the early 1900s, as desire for independence grew, numerous revolts broke out in Indonesia, especially in Java. The Dutch put down these revolts with great bloodshed. During World War II (1939–1945), the Japanese army occupied Indonesia and violently repressed the liberation movements. After the Japanese were expelled from the archipelago at the end of the war, the revolts erupted again. In 1945 the nationalist leader Sukarno proclaimed the Republic of Indonesia. The Netherlands acknowledged

Indonesia's independence in 1949.

Indonesia faced bloody internal struggles after gaining self-rule. Sukarno resigned after a failed overthrow of the government in 1965. Since then Suharto has led a strict government regime that has faced frequent upheavals.

Key Facts
- The first great Indonesian kingdoms arose in the fourth century A.D.
- The Dutch arrived in Indonesia in the 1600s.

49

Cultural Life

The Tradition of the Buffalo and the Bull

Bovines—a group of animals including oxen and buffalo—have long been an important part of life in Indonesia. The animals appear in the earliest written texts.

Strong, easy to train, and peaceful, buffalo can work under any conditions and are essential to rice cultivation. Linked to religion and to war, bulls appeared later in Indonesian legends.

Famous Bulls

Bulls have had religious and economic importance in Indonesia for 1,500 years. On Sumatra, the Minangkabau people live in houses with roofs shaped like horns. They even call themselves the "bull people." According to legend, these people won their freedom when their sacred bull won a combat against the bull of the Javanese kingdom of Mataram.

Cattle are used as currency to negotiate wedding dowries, as contracts between property owners, and as payment for injuries. On the island of Sulawesi, the Toraja people still practice the buffalo cult, in which the animal is considered to be the vehicle for ancestors and higher powers to communicate with the living.

The horns of sacrificial bulls are a sign of wealth among the Toraja.

The Ancient Tradition of the Bull

The "region of the bulls" is home to a unique competition—bull racing. Famous throughout the islands, these races are central to the ancient bull culture.

Certain buffalo and bulls have always been kept apart for racing rather than for working in the fields. Considered warriors, these racing animals symbolize strength and courage. All societies in the "region of the bulls" have made bovines part of their rituals and have given special status to them and to the people who work with the animals.

The tradition of raising the animals passes from father to son. The region's most famous ranches are in southern Madura, eastern Java, and the Negara region of Bali. Buffalo and bulls from these areas are trained either for combat or for racing.

The monument to the right stands in the Negara region of Bali, where the best mekepung drivers are greatly admired.

Heroes

To win a bull race, owners sometimes go into debt to obtain the fastest animals. Monuments are built in the center of villages to honor great victories or to celebrate famous drivers.

51

Races

The **grumbunggan,** the mekepung on Bali, and the kerapan sapi on Madura are the three major races. All are linked to Indonesian agricultural rites of sowing and harvesting crops.

The grumbunggan is the least violent of the races. It takes place just after the harvests in the Singaradja region of northern Bali. Colorfully decorated oxen are harnessed to magnificent wagons mounted on wooden rollers. The teams compete during a demonstration event in which they must "dance" with their heads and tails held high. The jury judges their performance according to speed, but the elegance of the wagon and team are also taken into account in choosing the winner.

The mekepung race is based on speed and the ability to move with ease and grace. Buffalo are selected by color, which varies from pink to gray-brown. The animals are harnessed to small, lightweight wagons, each of which is decorated with the colors of the owners. The animals are presented to the gods in ritual fashion. Their horns are

Passing a competitor is dangerous in the mekepung race.

Victory or Defeat

The winning animal brings glory and wealth to its owner. But a series of losses can mean the rapid loss of hard-earned social status or even banishment from the village and loss of all property.

Key Facts

- Buffalo and bulls have been at the center of Indonesian culture for centuries.
- The buffalo is mainly a working farm animal.
- Bulls participate in special ceremonies and races.

painted, and bells are hung around their necks. The races are run on narrow paths that wind through the rice paddies. The final race is held near Negara.

The kerapan sapi is the most important—and the most violent—of the three races. The kerapan kapubaten (elimination races) begin in April, and the championship race takes place in October in the small town of Pamekasan on Madura.

A strap covered with sharp points is attached to the bull's tail.

The powerful, half-wild bulls are harnessed to a simple shaft on which the driver—usually a young boy—balances. At the starting signal, the animals' sides and hindquarters are whipped with iron-tipped rods. The pain enrages the animals, who throw themselves forward and run for 100 to 200 yards. These animals, which weigh almost 1,000 pounds, can reach speeds of more than 40 miles per hour. After crossing the finish line, the driver must leap over the shaft and jump onto the necks of his bulls to stop them. Every year, drivers and spectators are injured or even killed.

Islam is the dominant religion in Indonesia, although a few islands retain their own forms of worship.

Islam in Indonesia
A Peaceful and Late Arrival

The religion of Islam, which originated on the Arabian Peninsula of the Middle East, did not dominate Indonesia until the 1500s. Long before that, however, Arab traders had come to the islands seeking spices, sandalwood and other precious woods, as well as fragrant resins such as benzoin. These early traders did not try to convert the local population, so the new faith spread very slowly. By the late 1200s, the Italian explorer Marco Polo noted the existence of small sultanates (regions governed by sultans) in northern Sumatra.

When the king of Malacca in Malaysia converted to Islam in the 1400s, the religion began to spread. The king transformed his capital into an international trading center and put all his energy into the service of his new faith.

A Tradition of Tolerance

Until the 1800s, Islam in Indonesia tolerated the existence of other religious communities, such as animists, Buddhists, and Hindus. Over time Islam gradually absorbed the other religions but kept some of their customs and rituals. Islam as practiced in Indonesia is a result of this continual mixture, and close to 90 percent of the nation's people are Muslims.

Indonesia and the Muslim World

Some conservative Muslims, called fundamentalists, do not like the form of Islam practiced in Indonesia. Since the 1970s, for example, countries such as Saudi Arabia and the United Arab Emirates—which have loaned money to Indonesia— have pressured the government to give in to the demands of Muslim fundamentalists on Sumatra and Java. Indonesian policy continues to take into account the demands of the international Muslim community.

Sculpture from the main temple of Prambanan, Java.

Pre-Islamic Influences

Aside from a few areas controlled by Muslims, Islamic law is not strictly applied in Indonesia. On eastern Java, Hinduism underlies the entire culture. On Bali 75 percent of the people are Hindus.

Ancient animist religions survive on many other islands, including Sumatra, Kalimantan, the Moluccas, Timor, and Irian Jaya. Although Indonesia has the largest Muslim population in the world, modern sultans on Java still worship gods of the earth and the sea.

Key Facts

- Islam has been the main religion in Indonesia since the 1500s.
- Islam in Indonesia exists alongside other religions still practiced in the country.

The ancient temple at Borobudur, Java, is one of many traces of Buddhism in Indonesia.

The Future

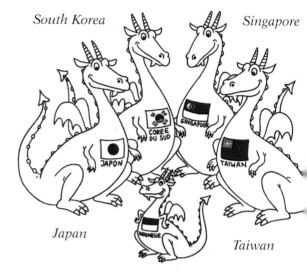

South Korea

Singapore

Japan

Taiwan

Indonesia

The Shift in World Power

Countries of the Pacific Ocean region—including Japan, Taiwan, South Korea, and Singapore—have enjoyed increasing international economic influence since the 1980s. Australia is also becoming a significant political and economic force, especially since the collapse of the former Soviet Union in 1991. With immense natural and human potential, Indonesia hopes to join these Pacific powerhouses.

A Strategic Location

The world's major trading nations are very interested in Indonesia. Situated between India, China, and Australia, the Indonesian archipelago has a strategic location for trade. Indonesia has also become a leading member of the Association of Southeast Asian Nations (ASEAN), a political organization that Japan, Europe, and the United States must take seriously.

Future Challenges

Although Indonesia will likely play a major international role in the 21st century, several problems face the nation.

The country uses U.S. dollars to buy foreign goods and to pay foreign debts. But the value of the dollar has dropped, so Indonesia has to spend more money to purchase imports and to pay its debts. This situation has burdened the national budget. With a rate of inflation close to 10 percent and a foreign debt of $82 billion, Indonesia's economic situation is critical.

Additional challenges facing Indonesia are unemployment, underemployment, and the increase in religious fundamentalism.

With a rapidly growing population, most Indonesians do not enjoy a high standard of living.

The Indonesian government has difficulty balancing its economic and political needs with the demands of nationalists and fundamentalists. Recent conflicts with other Islamic nations have caused some countries to fear that the Muslim influence in Indonesia will override the country's commercial interests. As a result of these concerns, major trading powers hesitate to invest more heavily in Indonesia.

Population growth and urban overcrowding are two serious challenges facing Indonesia.

Glossary

archipelago (arh-kuh-PEH-luh-goh) A chain, or group, of islands scattered throughout a large expanse of water.

gamelan (GA-muh-lan) An Indonesian orchestra made up of metal gongs, bamboo flutes, xylophones, drums, and stringed instruments. The orchestras perform at religious ceremonies, shadow plays, village festivals, hotels, and nightclubs.

grumbunggan (groom-BOONG-uhn) An ox race in the northern part of the island of Bali in which the animals are harnessed to a wagon and are judged on speed and elegance.

kerapan sapi (kuh-RAH-pahn SAH-pee) A bull race on the island of Madura in which the animals are harnessed to a single shaft on which a young driver must balance during the course of the race. At the finish line, the driver leaps over the shaft onto the bulls' necks to stop the animals, who may be running as fast as 40 miles per hour.

Malay (muh-LAY) A member of a people of the Malay Peninsula, eastern Sumatra, parts of the island of Borneo, and some nearby islands.

mekepung (MUH-kuh-poong) A buffalo race in which the animals are gaily decorated and harnessed to small wagons. The race is run through the rice paddies of western Bali.

monsoon (mahn-soon) A seasonal wind that blows over the northern Indian Ocean, bringing heavy rains to the coastal and island regions of southern Asia. Monsoons blow from the southwest between April and October and from the northeast between November and March.

Negrito (nuh-GREE-toh) A member of a group of small, dark-skinned people who live in the central and southern Pacific region as well as in Southeast Asia.

Index

Acknowledgments

All photos by Alain Chenevière except the following: D. R., pp. 47, 48; Musée national d'histoire naturelle (France), p. 46; Musée de la marine (France), p. 49; Artwork by Anne Bodin, pp. 40–41, 42, 51; Artwork by Natacha Kotlarevsky, pp. 4–24; Charts by Emmanuel Calamy, pp. 43, 44; Maps by Patrick Mérienne, pp. 38–39, 40